HOW? WHO? WHAT? WHEN? WHERE? WHY?

Questions kids ask

ABOUT
THEMSELVES

Copyright © 1988 by Grolier Limited

ISBN 0-7172-4631-0
ISBN 0-7172-4626-4 (set)

Printed and manufactured in the United States of America.

Questions Kids Ask... about THEMSELVES

continued

What is a belly button?

It is on your belly. But it's not a button. Your belly button is what is left of the tube that once joined you to your mother. This tube is called an umbilical cord. You don't remember being attached to your mother because it was before you were born, when you were growing inside your mother's body.

The umbilical cord brought you all the food and oxygen you needed. Your mother ate and breathed for you. Digested food from your mother's body came to you through this tube. When your mother took a breath of air, she used some of it and sent the rest to you. When you were born the cord was cut and you had to begin breathing and eating on your own.

For the rest of your life your belly button will remind you of the time before you were born.

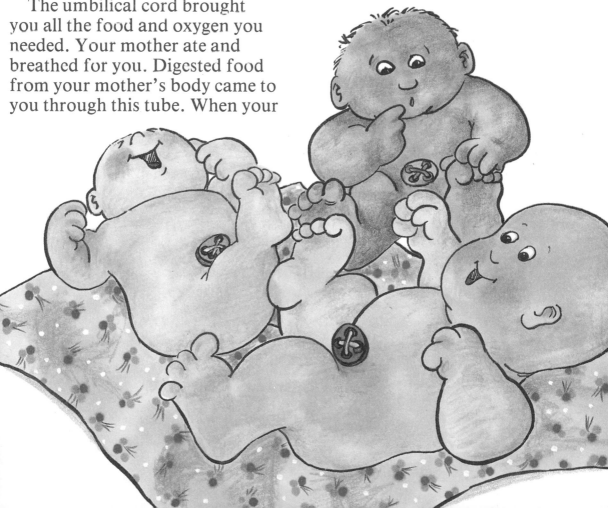

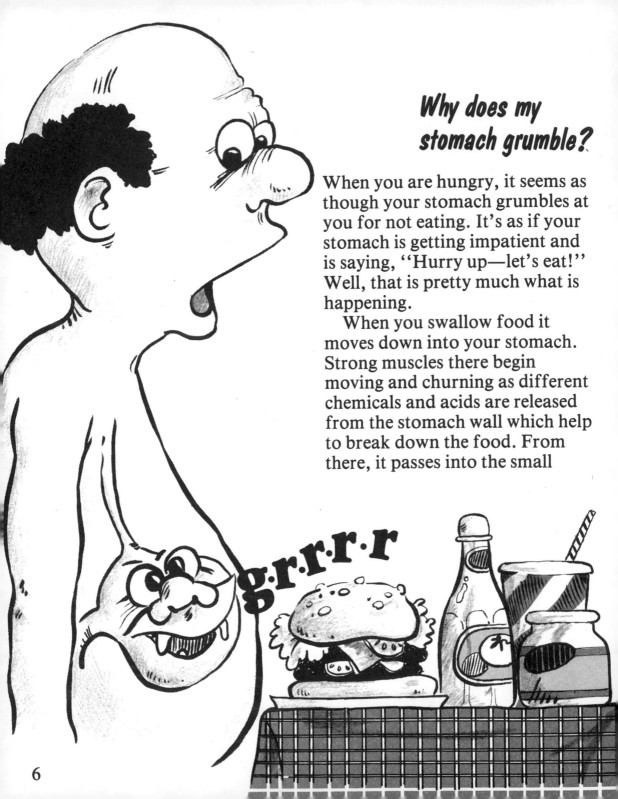

Why does my stomach grumble?

When you are hungry, it seems as though your stomach grumbles at you for not eating. It's as if your stomach is getting impatient and is saying, "Hurry up—let's eat!" Well, that is pretty much what is happening.

When you swallow food it moves down into your stomach. Strong muscles there begin moving and churning as different chemicals and acids are released from the stomach wall which help to break down the food. From there, it passes into the small

g·r·r·r·r

intestine where the goodness of the food is absorbed into your body.

Your stomach has a very good memory. It gets used to eating at the same times each day and it produces acids and chemicals and starts churning right on time. If there is no food to absorb all this activity, your stomach makes a lot of noise.

So if your stomach thinks it's lunchtime and you haven't eaten yet, you'll hear your stomach complaining. And rightly so—it's hungry.

DID YOU KNOW . . . it takes 48 hours for your body to completely digest one meal!

How long can you go without eating or drinking?

How long you can last without eating depends on how big you are to start with and how healthy. In general, people can last a surprisingly long time without food. The longest recorded time someone has gone without eating is 382 days. That's more than a year! But most people wouldn't last nearly that long. Many adults can fast, or go without food, for periods of about six weeks without hurting themselves.

Going without water, however, is a different matter. The longest recorded time that someone has survived without food or water is only 18 days. And this was considered to be a surprisingly long time. Most of us wouldn't last a week without water.

What's so funny about your "funny bone"?

Have you ever whacked the back of your elbow and felt a painful, tingling feeling run down your arm? Someone tells you you've hit your "funny bone," but what's so funny about it?— you're in pain!

"Funny bone" is just an expression. In fact, it isn't even a bone! Your "funny bone" is a nerve at the back of your elbow just above the bone. The nerve lies near the surface of your skin so it's not as protected as other nerves in your body. Even a light bump on the nerve causes pain and a tingling feeling that travels down your arm into your ring finger and pinky.

The misleading name "funny bone" may have come from a word play on "humerus," the large bone in your upper arm.

ha·ha·ha·ha!

What's the biggest bone in my body?

The biggest bone in your body is your thigh bone, or femur. This bone stretches from your hip down to your knee. It is the longest and heaviest bone you have. The femur is also the strongest bone because it carries the weight of your body and must support your leg muscles, which are very powerful.

What's the smallest bone in my body?

The bones in your body come in all shapes and sizes. The very smallest bone is no bigger than a grain of rice. This bone is called the stapes, or stirrup, and is deep inside your ear. The stapes helps to carry sound through your ear to your brain so that you can hear. Without it you would be deaf. So even the smallest parts of your body have important jobs to do!

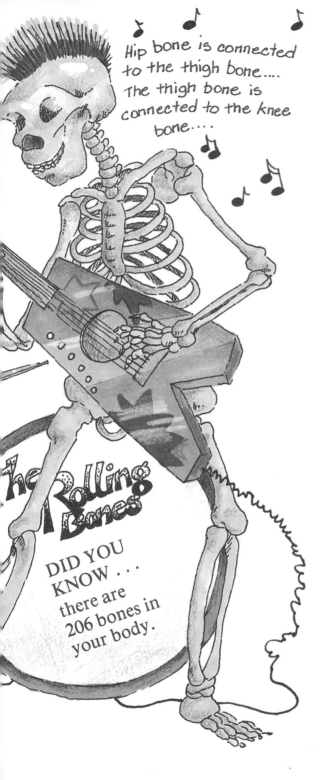

Hip bone is connected to the thigh bone.... The thigh bone is connected to the knee bone....

The Rolling Bones

DID YOU KNOW ... there are 206 bones in your body.

What holds my bones together?

As the song says, all your bones are connected to each other. And all these connected bones make up your skeleton, the frame of your body.

The skeleton is very strong because the connections between the bones are strong too. The place where one bone is connected to another is called a joint. Most joints, such as your knees and fingers, move. A few, such as those between the bones in your skull, don't move at all.

Joints that don't move have nothing between the bones, or only a thin layer of tissue. In moveable joints the bones are firmly attached to each other by ligaments. These are bands of tissue that are as strong as rope. Sometimes these ligaments get twisted or torn, causing a sprain. The ligament swells up and gets stiff, making it very painful when you try to move it. But the nice thing about ligaments is that they heal all by themselves, usually as good as new.

Why do we sleep?

Sleep is one of the great mysteries of life. Humans as well as most animals need to sleep every day. Sleep restores energy to your body, especially to your brain and nervous system. It also gives your body a chance to repair itself.

Basically, there are two kinds of sleep. During one kind, called slow-wave sleep, you don't dream and your brain slows down. But during what is called REM (rapid eye movement) sleep, you dream and your brain is very active. You have both kinds of sleep several times each night.

Sleep is so mysterious that scientists still don't know much about it. They don't know what each kind of sleep really does or how sleep recharges your body with energy.

What are dreams?

A dream is an imaginary story that goes on in your mind when you are asleep. Some dreams

seem very real. You can see, taste, hear, touch and smell in a dream, and most dreams are in color.

We all dream, usually for about 100 minutes over 8 hours sleep. Often we don't remember our dreams, and sometimes we remember only parts of a dream.

Where does the story of a dream come from? It's made up in your mind. A dream is usually about things you've done and feelings you've had the day before. It can also be based on your wishes, which often come true in your dreams. If you wish you were a rock star, you just might dream that you are one!

How long can you go without sleep?

So you want to stay up late? How long do you think you can stay up? An hour might be fun, but what about two days?

You can live quite awhile without sleep, but eventually you would not be able to do even simple things. After one night without sleep you would be grouchy and slow. After two nights you would be unable to concentrate and do easy tasks like reciting the alphabet. After three days without sleep you would have trouble thinking, seeing and hearing. Even speaking a sentence would be difficult.

People have stayed awake for as long as eleven days. After such a long time without sleep they become confused and no longer know what is real and what isn't.

Everything seems like a frightening nightmare. At this point they usually scream or cry and then collapse into a deep sleep on the nearest floor.

Now, how long was it that you wanted to stay up past your bedtime?

Why aren't all people the same color?

Some people have black skin, others have white skin and still others have a yellowish tone to their skin. Everyone's skin has an outside layer called the epidermis. Inside the epidermis is a coloring material called melanin. The more melanin in your skin, the darker you are.

Your skin color has much to do with which part of the world your ancestors originally came from. The ancestors of people with dark skin lived in hot countries where there was a lot of sunshine. Their skin became dark to protect them from the sun's hot rays. The people who lived in cooler, northern countries were exposed to less sun, so their skin color was very light.

Skin colors were passed along generation after generation. People moved to different climates all over the world; but no matter what climate people live in, their skin color is determined by where their ancestors lived in times past.

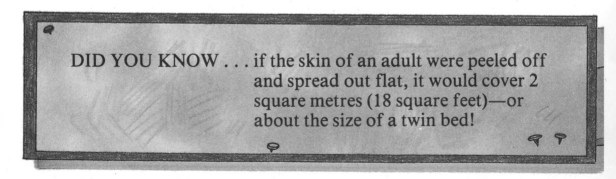

DID YOU KNOW . . . if the skin of an adult were peeled off and spread out flat, it would cover 2 square metres (18 square feet)—or about the size of a twin bed!

Is there invisible life on our bodies?

You may be surprised to discover that an invisible zoo lives on your body! The surface of your skin hides a miniature world of tiny animals too small to see except through a microscope. Magnified hundreds of times, these tiny creatures look like little dinosaurs.

One kind that we know of are tiny mites called "Demodex Follicularum," which live in the roots of our eyelashes. They cause no harm, but scientists are still trying to discover why they are there and what they do. We do know that one of their favorite foods is mascara!

Why do I have toes?

Curl your toes under and try to walk. It's hard, isn't it? You can walk smoothly because your toes let your foot bend. Without them you would only be able to clump along slowly. Your toes also help you keep your balance. The spread of five separate toes means your foot can handle your shifting weight as you move. Without toes you would be in danger of falling over even when you were just standing.

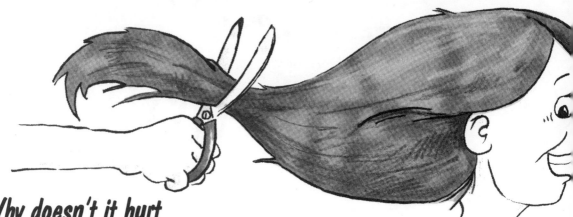

Why doesn't it hurt to get a haircut?

Hair doesn't have any feeling. There is no nerve pathway between your hair and your brain, so you can't feel your hair being cut.

However there are many nerves in the skin around the root of each hair. These nerves let you feel any movement of your hair. So, it may not hurt to have your hair cut, but it sure hurts to have your hair pulled!

How does your hair grow?

Each hair on your head has a root and a shaft. When you brush or comb your hair, it's the hair shaft that you're styling. The root of your hair is a soft, light-colored bulb below the surface of your scalp. It lies in a casing called the follicle. At the bottom of the follicle is the papilla, which nourishes the root.

Your hair grows when new cells form around the papilla. These new cells push up on the old cells, gradually forcing them up out of the follicle. The old cells are now part of the shaft. As long as the papilla provides nourishment for new cells, your hair continues to grow. The papilla can nourish new cells for years.

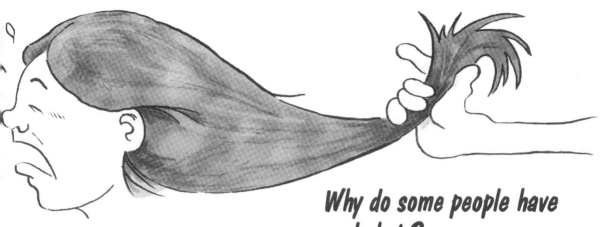

Why do we have hair?

The hair on our heads helps keep us warm and protects us from head injuries. The hairs in our eyebrows, eyelashes, nostrils and ears act as filters, helping to keep out dust and other irritating particles.

Most mammals have a thick coat of hair all over which does a good job of keeping them warm. When they feel cold, muscles in their skin contract and make the hair stand on end, forming a thick barrier which helps keep warm air near the body. You may have noticed that when you get cold, "goose bumps" pop up on your skin. These little bumps are actually tiny muscles holding your hair erect in an effort to warm you too.

Why do some people have curly hair?

Some people have a hard time getting their hair to curl, while others cannot make their hair lie straight no matter how hard they try. The difference lies in the shape of the individual hairs.

If you were to pull out one of your hairs, slice it crosswise and look at it under a microscope, you would see that it is one of three shapes.

If you have straight hair, the cross section will be round. If your hair is wavy, the shape is oval. Kinky hair has more of a cupped shape.

Hairs that are not round tend to grow at an uneven rate in different places, and this is what makes them go curly!

ROUND   OVAL   CUPPED

What are nerves?

Can you imagine life without the telephone? How would you send messages quickly? Your body has a telephone system too. The nervous system is a communication network that lets almost every part of your body send messages to another part.

Nerves are the telephone lines of this system. They are made up of bundles of nerve cells that carry information as electrical impulses. Some nerves are pathways to the brain, and others

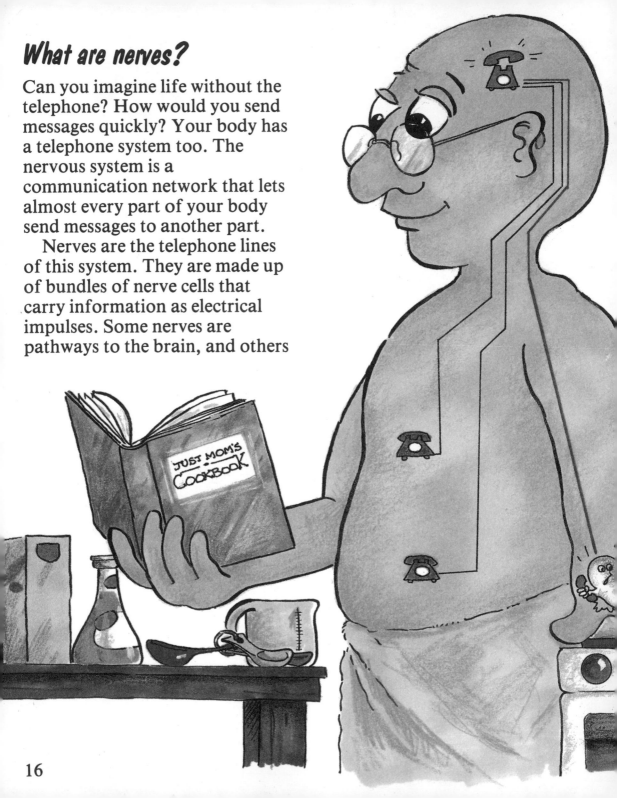

are pathways from the brain. Some help you feel cold, heat, pain and pressure. Other nerves tell parts of your body to move.

Your nerves send messages very quickly. For example, let's say you burn your hand. The pain and heat nerves in your hand send a message to your brain. Your brain answers back along different nerves that the muscles in your arm should jerk your hand away. This all takes less than one second. Information travels along your nerves at between 1 and 100 metres (3 and 300 feet) per second!

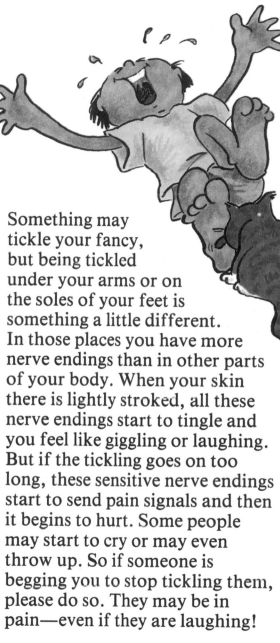

Something may tickle your fancy, but being tickled under your arms or on the soles of your feet is something a little different. In those places you have more nerve endings than in other parts of your body. When your skin there is lightly stroked, all these nerve endings start to tingle and you feel like giggling or laughing. But if the tickling goes on too long, these sensitive nerve endings start to send pain signals and then it begins to hurt. Some people may start to cry or may even throw up. So if someone is begging you to stop tickling them, please do so. They may be in pain—even if they are laughing!

What do tonsils do?

If your tonsils have ever been infected, you know how miserable they can make you feel. What you don't know is that tonsils become infected because of the job they do.

Tonsils are located in the walls of your throat on either side of the uvula, the piece of tissue that hangs down at the back of your mouth. Their job is to make white blood cells to fight the germs that get into your body through your mouth. Unfortunately a great many germs get in that way, and your tonsils can't always fight them all successfully. As a result, they may get infected themselves. Children have much bigger tonsils than adults do, so their tonsils get infected more often.

Tonsils that get infected all the time need to be taken out. This is a simple operation called a tonsillectomy. But if you lose your tonsils, don't worry—your body has many other defenses.

How do we taste?

Would you rather have a big bowl of brussel sprouts or a slice of chocolate cake? Taste is something that your brain decides. The tongue's job is to send information about the food in your mouth to your brain.

Your tongue is covered with tiny taste buds that are made up of small receptor cells. The taste buds are bunched up into bumps called papillae. If you stick out your tongue and look at it in a mirror, you can see small bumps all over it. These are the papillae.

As you chew, the receptor cells send information about the food to two main nerves, one attached to the front of your tongue, the other to the sides and back. The information travels along these nerves to the brain, which sorts it all out and tells you what the food tastes like.

Every twenty days you grow a new set of receptor cells. Your taste may change too as you get older. Some day, you may even like brussel sprouts more than chocolate cake!

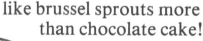

Why do baby teeth fall out?

You have about twenty baby teeth, just the right number for the size of your mouth. But as you grow, your mouth gets bigger, and so you need bigger teeth and more of them.

When you are about four years old, your permanent teeth start growing near the roots of your baby teeth. As they grow, they cause the roots of the baby teeth to dissolve. When the root is completely dissolved the tooth loosens and falls out, and your permanent tooth comes in.

It takes a long time to get all your permanent teeth. The first baby tooth falls out when you are six or seven, and they keep falling out until you are almost a teenager. As you lose each baby tooth, a permanent tooth takes its place.

The last to come in are molars at the very back of your mouth. They are called wisdom teeth because they don't appear until you are between eighteen and twenty years old.

How do I see?

Imagine that you couldn't see! Your eyes let you read, watch television, play games, and do thousands of other things.

When light hits an object, the light rays bounce back and enter your eye through the pupil, the black dot in the middle of the colored iris. The rays then go through the lens, which bends them into a small point of light that hits the retina at the back of your eyeball.

The retina is a small piece of tissue covered with small cones and rods that turn the light into electrical signals. These signals then travel along the optic nerve to the brain, and the brain turns the signals into an image that you can understand.

Where do tears come from?

Each time you blink, a little salty water washes over your eyes to keep them wet. We call that water, tears. Tears are produced in glands under your eyelids and come out through small holes. When you are sad or laughing hard, the muscles around these holes squeeze tight. This makes the tears rush out, and so your eyes fill up with water.

When you cry, the tears that don't splash down your cheeks run down the inside of your nose.

DID YOU KNOW . . . your eyes "see" things upside down. Your brain turns images right side up!

Why do we blink?

Blinking is something you do all the time, although you usually aren't aware of it. Try counting the number of times you blink in a minute. The average person blinks about 25 times a minute!

There are two reasons for blinking. The first is to keep the surface of your eye clean and to protect it against any object that suddenly comes toward it.

The second reason has to do with the way you are feeling. Blinking among primates (monkeys, apes and humans) is believed to be a way of communicating stress. In other words, if you are worried or upset you tend to blink more.

Blinking or winking can also convey friendliness—but in this case, of course, it is something you do on purpose.

What are freckles?

If you have blond or red hair, you have probably moaned about having freckles. But those small, light brown flecks are a natural part of your skin.

Everyone's skin makes a pigment called melanin that protects you from the sun and helps prevent sunburn. Sometimes the melanin builds up in spots, and those spots form freckles.

People with very light skin and blond or red hair are most likely to get freckles because they are more sensitive to sunlight. Your face and hands are the most prone to freckles because they are the parts of your body that get the most sun.

How old could you live to be?

The oldest person ever was Shigechiyo Izumi, who died in 1986 at the age of 120. He lived on the island of Tokunoshima in Japan. A retired dock worker, he said he lived so long because of his "simple diet." Few people alive today will reach that age. But never mind: 300 years ago, people in North America and Europe didn't expect to live much longer than 35 or 40 years!

These days, 40 is still young, and lots of people are still enjoying life at age 70. What accounts for the difference? A lot of things, but especially what we have learned in the meantime about diseases and good eating habits.

As we learn more, we may well increase the chance of people living even longer. By understanding how and why we age, scientists think they may be able to slow down the process. Unfortunately, it looks as if stopping it entirely is still an impossible dream.

Why do we age?

In an old Greek story a god punishes a man by giving him eternal life, but not eternal youth. The man just grows older and older forever.

Growing old is a natural part of life. When you are young, your body grows bigger and stronger. But after sixty years or so, your body starts to wear down, just like a machine does after many years of use. Your senses grow weaker, your movement slows down, and your energy level becomes lower. Your brain ages better than the rest of your body. Unless you have a brain disease or injury, you will be as smart and alert in your old age as you are now.

How do people grow?

Every part of your body is made up of billions of cells. Your skin, teeth and hair, your muscles, nerves, bones and blood are all made of cells. Look at your finger. Do you see any cells? No. Cells are so small that you can only see them through a microscope.

Cells are like bricks. When they are put together with other materials, they can build bodies. When you are born, your body is small. It does not have many cells. When you eat and drink, you feed your cells. They grow bigger. Then each cell divides. It becomes two cells. Then these cells grow and divide. They make even more cells. As these new cells are being made, your body is growing!

DID YOU KNOW . . . your brain will stop growing in size when you are 15 years old!

How tall will I grow?

How tall you will grow depends mainly on two things. A healthy diet will help you to grow tall. But the most important thing is the height of your parents. If they are short, you will probably be short; and if they are tall you will probably be tall too. If one of your parents is short and the other is tall, it is harder to guess how tall you will grow. Normally, a six-year-old boy and a five-year-old girl are two-thirds of their adult height. But not always. So don't be surprised if it turns out that the smallest person in your classroom grows up to be the tallest adult.

Jan. 1
Nov 9
June 30
May 4
Jan. 1
Nov. 14
Sept. 2
May 4
Dec. 1

What happens when I blush?

Have you ever felt embarrassed and suddenly found that your cheeks had turned bright red and warm? You were blushing, of course. But why does your face have to look and feel like a thermometer?

Blood flows to the skin through tiny blood vessels called capillaries. Each capillary has nerves which control the flow of blood to the surface of the skin. When you are embarrassed these nerves cause the capillaries to suddenly expand and fill with blood, making your cheeks turn bright red. Shame, nervousness, excitement and other emotions can also cause you to blush.

Why do I sweat when I'm hot?

After running hard on a hot day, your body is covered with sweat. But did you know that you sweat, or perspire, in very small amounts all the time?

Your body likes to be at one constant temperature —37.0° C or 98.6° F—and it's always making

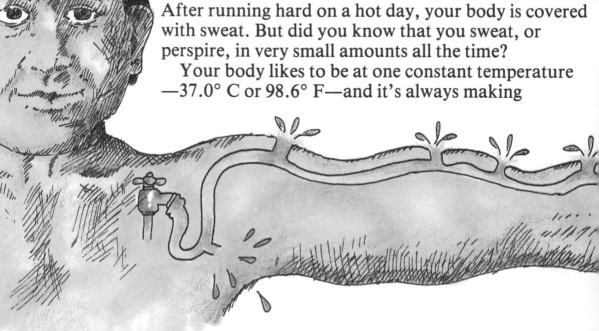

What is a fever?

Perhaps the worst part about being sick is having a fever. You feel hot, tired, thirsty and headachy. Worse still, your mother or father usually makes you stay in bed for a couple of days.

There are many causes of fever, but the most common one is an infection. As your body fights the infection, it makes more heat than usual, and you get a fever.

Doctors also believe that some diseases confuse the part of your brain that controls your body's temperature, and that this causes fever too.

Fevers are not usually serious. But in some diseases a fever can go so high that it becomes very dangerous indeed. Fortunately, most people have had shots to prevent these diseases.

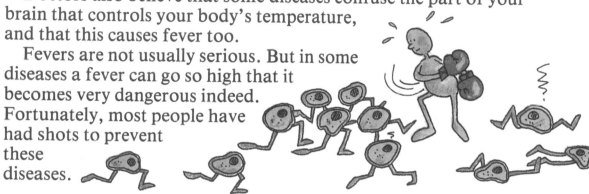

adjustments to stay there. Sweating is the way your body releases excess heat to stay cool.

The surface of your body is covered with sweat glands. There are larger ones under your arms, on the palms of your hands, and on the soles of your feet.

When your body cools itself, these glands cover your skin with a salty water. As the sweat evaporates your body becomes cooler.

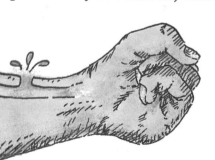

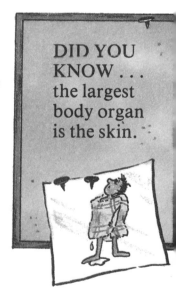

DID YOU KNOW . . . the largest body organ is the skin.

How do we hear?

Hold your hands tightly over your ears. Notice how sounds become dull? Your ears are certainly more than just holes in your head. They are complex organs of hearing.

Sound travels as invisible waves in the air. These waves enter your ear and strike a thin, stretched piece of tissue called the eardrum. As the eardrum begins to vibrate, it causes three small bones in your middle ear to vibrate. This, in turn, causes the liquid in the snail-shaped part of your inner ear called the cochlea to vibrate too.

The vibrating liquid causes small hairs to bend. As they bend, they send impulses along the nerve to your brain. Finally, your brain changes these impulses to sounds that you can understand.

Sound also travels through your skull. For example, you hear your own voice mainly from inside your head, so your voice sounds different to you than it does to other people. Listen to your voice on a tape recorder. You'll be surprised at how different you sound!

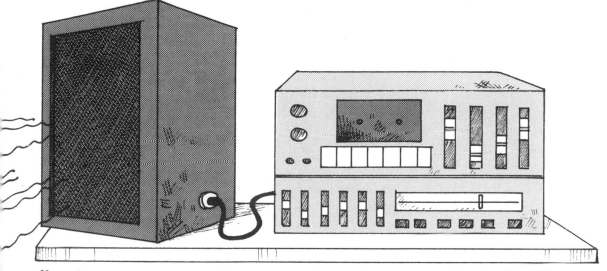

Why do you get dizzy?

If you spin around rapidly you get dizzy. What causes this funny feeling? Would you believe your ears? Not the part you can see, but the part known as the "inner ear."

The inner ear has three loops filled with liquid, known as the "semicircular canals." Each canal has tiny hairs growing at the bottom of it. The hairs are connected to nerves, which carry messages to your brain about the position of the hairs.

When you move, the liquid swishes back and forth and presses against the hairs, making them bend. Then the brain knows enough to tighten this muscle and relax that one so that you can keep your balance.

When you twirl, the liquid moves rapidly back and forth over these hairs and your brain gets confusing information. As a result you feel off-balance. Fortunately, the liquid soon settles down and your brain gets your muscles working properly.

Can you read another person's mind?

Have you ever known what other people were thinking before they told you? Perhaps it's just a coincidence. On the other hand, it may be that you are receiving their thoughts by using mental telepathy. In other words, you may be reading their minds!

Scientists are still studying mental telepathy. Most scientists do not believe that it exists. Others believe that mental telepathy is real and that a person's thoughts can be read by another person in the same room, the same city or as far away as across the world!

Now close your eyes and think hard about a big slice of cake.

If someone is reading your mind, that person might already be bringing you one right now.

Would the person with the largest brain be the smartest person in the world?

If you had a bigger brain you wouldn't be any smarter. It's not the size of your brain that makes you smart. What makes you smart is the way that your brain develops.

Your brain stores information about your past experiences. This is why you can learn, remember and think. Some people don't do these things as quickly as others. It could be because they don't have as great a capacity for learning, or because they aren't in an environment that helps them to learn. But it has nothing to do with the size of their brain.

In fact, most adult brains are the same size.

Is a brain smarter than a computer?

Computers are amazing machines. They can play chess, design a bridge, or solve a math problem. But even though they can do all this, computers are not as smart as the human brain. A computer can compute and analyze data, but a computer cannot really *think*.

A computer knows and does only what you tell it. Basically, it just follows the rules in its program. But your brain gathers new information and then uses it to figure out things that you did not know before. This is called creative thinking or invention.

For example, your brain could figure out how to tie a shoelace or how to invent a new breakfast cereal. But a computer couldn't— not even if it had hands and ate breakfast cereal every morning!

Your brain does hundreds of things at once. It keeps your body working, tells you to move, thinks, lets you see, hear and feel. Your brain is very smart indeed.

What is a "charley horse"?

Charley Horse sounds like someone's name, doesn't it? But a charley horse isn't a person. It's the name given to a muscle condition.

Have you ever been playing or running when all of a sudden one of your muscles became stiff and sore? You could very well have had a charley horse. They occur most often in leg muscles, usually after you've stretched and strained the muscle. For a few days the muscle can feel cramped, and there could even be some swelling if the muscle fibers have been torn.

Why do they call it a charley horse? The muscle pain was named after the old work horses that hauled heavy farm equipment. When a horse became lame and could no longer work, it was called a charley horse. People began to use this expression to describe their own overused, sore muscles.

I GUESS I'M RIGHTHANDED!

Why are some people left-handed?

A story in the Bible says that Jesus sits at God's right hand. Since then people have believed that right was the good side and left was the bad. Also, because so few people used their left hands, being left-handed was thought unlucky. To this day we still take oaths and shake with our right hands.

But we know now that it is your brain that decides if you are right-handed or left-handed. Your brain is made up of two halves that are joined by a thick tube of nerves. Scientists have discovered that right-handed people usually have their speech controlled on the left side of their brain while left-handed people have it on the right side or both sides.

Why do we hiccup?

Nobody seems to know. Hiccups have no use that anyone can figure out. Hiccupping is a little like vomiting, because your stomach tightens in spasms for both. But everything else is different. In hiccupping, you suck in air and your diaphragm tightens. Your diaphragm is the layer of muscle that separates your lungs from your stomach. Often you start to hiccup when you've eaten too quickly, or if you've eaten something with lots of hot pepper.

Hiccupping is a reflex, which means that it is something that our body does on its own. We don't tell a reflex to work, and usually we can't stop it. To get rid of the hiccups you can try breathing into a paper bag or drinking a glass of water without stopping for a breath.

Some people get the hiccups so badly that they have them for days, and may even die of exhaustion. Fortunately, most people stop hiccupping after a few minutes.

Index